all the things i
never meant to mean

ginger h. goodall

ISBN: 979-8-9910854-0-3
Cover design by: Ginger H. Goodall using Canva.com
Printed in the United States of America.

Contents

to my sister and mother

*thank you for giving me back the courage
to write out loud*

Blanketed in Sunshine

If depression is a blanket.
In the past it has weighed me down and
suffocated me... But now, every once in a while, it
envelopes me like a glass of warm milk on a
restless 1 a.m.

Something once so tragic
I find myself slipping back into every now and
again
just because it became home so long ago, for so
long
and now it holds so well as a fortress

depression takes the physicality of spiked, fire-
breathing dragons
burning me slightly but guarding me from reality
contains me safely until I feel like I can come out
again
the walls of sheets envelope me like glue on a
broken vase
depression collects me like a hug
it cuts me and loves me all the same
depression and I, we understand each other
we have a bond together
been through hell together
it has become my nest
the comfort, the familiarity
it's exhausting yet gives me a strange rest
the numbing pinch of it

the calming center of a tornado
that's what I find from a dip into depression
it engulfs me
with a slight whisper of insanity
it helps me to cry
when there is no real tragedy going on outside
only the remains from tragedies of before

a lump of coal in my throat
a certain constriction in my chest
all implanted by my own hand
grenades thrown gently into my own head
to explode quietly
insanity seeping through the cracks of my skull
from damage long ago
cracks only I can feel beneath my fingertips
only I can feel the implements on my heart
only I can hear the thrumming of my anxiety
pulsating on my wrists
slipping between the bones of my ribcage—that
thing
utterly useless armor
never guarded my heart from a thing
all the harm slithered in effortlessly
and squeezed my heart mercilessly
bleeding infinitely
always hurting just lightly
a reminder of the abuse it received a while ago
a poem from 2020.

all the things i never meant to mean

eleven

I Don't Belong Here

Take me to a better place
Where there's no disgrace
Where I belong
Oh, I've been waiting far too long
Tell me that I'm not too late

I bend my knees and
Begging please
I fall to the ground
Find me a path to where dreams
Come true
The stars smile
The water is clear and blue

Hugs are shared between the two
At the other end of the rainbow
The other side of life

Take me to a place where I'm safe and sound
To a place where I won't be found.

Fallen Star

It's okay... It's okay...
It's okay to hide once in a while,
To need a disguise.
To let a few tears
Slip past your eyes.

Even the stars don't always glow,
Even the moon hides,
And the clouds cry.

If every person is a star,
Some glow, and some not at all.
A falling star grants a wish.
A falling girl breaks her heart.
The light in her dulls
And her soul weeps with the clouds.
During the fall.
During it all.
She screams
And the lightning strikes.

But when she smiles
The whole sky beams twice as bright

Replenish Me

It hurts me and cures me
To see your smile
And not hear your laugh
It pains me to see someone else
Get what I've been yearning for
Look at me
Be mine
I am empty in the most important part of me
And it is agony
Please fill the gap
Replenish me
Fill me to my extremes
To my ends and corners
Come closer so I can whisper to your heart
And feel it flutter beneath me
Sharing heated breaths
I want to return the favor
Of happiness and smiles
And many tugs on my heart
To your heart and soul

ginger h. goodall

twelve

11:11

Can't make wishes come true,
Darling it's just make-believe
That we tell ourselves at night
So that we can sleep
And fight
And fight.

It's 11:12
I've missed my wish by sixty seconds
I can't see the stars
No birthday candles...

11:11, see you tomorrow
Wish on you again
Every day I await you
You pretty number
You sweet promise
Of a better day.

Admirer

Hand outstretched
Fingertips spread
Fill the space
Interlock with me
Let us intertwine
Be mine

Why can't I wake up to you?
Sip tea with you
And love you up close?

Why can't I hear you?
See your pretty face
And feel you?

I am invisible to you; transparent.
A thin layer of glass
And it hurts me when you look straight past

You don't know who I am
Why are you so far away?
Come closer

Why can't you hear me?
Come closer

Why can't you see me?
Come closer

Let me feel you under my fingertips
Caress your imperfections
And kiss your scars
Let my eyes make contact with yours

Give me a chance.

I am just another girl
Watching you from the crowd
I am just another girl
You're making proud
I am just another girl
Head over heels
For the tousled hair
And boyish charm
On her computer screen.

God

I had total faith in you
But then things started going wrong
and I felt you weren't doing what you were
supposed to
That tore me away...
I had less and less faith in you as I grew on
I know I was wrong,
But you can't blame me, God,
I was all alone.

Bars

Nothing is more restraining than bars you can't
touch by hand.
And nothing is more heartbreaking than when a
born fighter
Stops fighting.
I see bars surrounding me,
I feel bars suffocating me,
I see blank walls and paper sheets;
All these whites are blinding me.

Oh, I see bars surrounding me,
I feel bars suffocating me,
I feel the cold chilling my entirety.

I wish to see angels fly above me,
But this is all I'll ever see,
And this is all I'll ever be.
So, I'll sleep; where they can't get me,
I'll sleep, and you can take me.

Once Upon a Tragedy

Now I'll tell you a story about a little girl
Who wasn't really little at all.

She was sensitive and fragile
But no one took notice of it.
She was surrounded by people,
And she felt all alone.

Day and night,
All the things that gave her fright;
Fights, screams and tears

Even after all these years

She couldn't escape,
Even in her dreams.

She hates loud sounds and angry frowns
Even if it's over now,
She's still scared and nervous in anticipation
Maybe she needs just a little confirmation...
That things are okay
Even if it is
Just for today.

You Blink Fast When You're Angry

Why won't you understand me?
Why won't you listen?
Why don't you care how you're affecting me?

Don't you know I cry into my pillow at night
My tears are my pleas;
Please stop torturing me
My cries are my screams;
Why can't you hear me?

I'm scared;
Because you don't even see me

Please stop;
You're torturing me
You're hurting me
Permanently
I'm scarred with neglect

You want to keep my heart beating
But don't care to keep my tears from streaming
What do I have to do to make you realize
That just because my heartbeat is strong
It doesn't mean that I'm holding on

I wish I had something to drown out the sound
And when I look around, I can't help but frown

Maybe someday, I will be free.

But by that time, will it really matter to me?
I guess I'll just have to wait and see.

Goodnight

No one is here for me
So my tears never dry

There are countless meanings behind them
But no one tries
They don't know what goes on inside

I often play about;
Smiling and laughing
So no one seems to have a doubt
That I'm okay

Maybe one day, before the sun is gone
Maybe one day, before I lose all hope

Once again, I shall cuddle myself to sleep
As there is no one here but me
Once again, I'm all alone
Once again in this empty room
Goodnight, Goodnight;
I'll sleep off the pain until morning comes to sight.

Wings

I'm drawing wings on my shoulder blades
Hoping I can fly away

I drew them with detail
Hoping they could repair
All the pain that lingers there
All the bad flowing through the air

Come to life

Take cover of my back
Let there be no attack
Make me better

Come to life

Wings
I drew you with detail
Hoping you could repair
All that's wrong with me

God, Validate Me

Tell me that I'm alright
That my head's screwed on right
Tell me that I'm not too dangerous
That it's not too late to change my crazy ways

Tell me that I'm not too far gone
That I can still move on
Tell me that I can prove myself wrong
That I can stay strong

Tell me that you'll hold on
Bear with me

I'm sorry it took me so long
To realize I've been doing wrong

Tell me that I can stay strong
Please wait with me and stay with me

Take my hand, lead the way; guide me to you
Take away the evil that rest in me
Tell me that I'm still going to the promised heaven
That lay waiting

Please keep me calm and steady
Keep me from shaking

My soul is yours for the taking
After my last breath has been taken

Introductions

This is someone who's scared and scarred
Who struggles to look in the mirror
insecure and unsafe
Who refuses self-forgiveness
Has a touch of evil that likes to take over
This is someone who's afraid of dying
but wonders if they're already dead
Fighting a battle with themselves
with too many battle scars
and no one to kiss them away
This is someone who lost themselves on the wrong path
Who's scared of roads, ways, choices and decisions
Who struggles to sleep
This is someone who has no one.
Say hello.

Once Upon a Time I Broke My Own Heart

I broke it, I smashed it, I tore it to pieces
And locked it away
Above fire and lava

The shards are sharp
Pieces fragile
I need you
To gather them

Put it back together
And cradle it to yours
But your hands will bleed
And I don't want to see
You ever hurt
Because of me.

Sister

I can feel your scars that no one sees
I dry the tears you've shed for years
I hear your pleas when your mouth is shut
I see blood from your cuts after they've healed
I see the tear stains on the pillowcase after they've
dried
I see that in the dark, your eyes are wide
I hear the scratch of pencil on your journal
Thoughts you're scared to say out loud
How you still haven't recovered from those jerks

But I know that you will show them all.
Close your eyes and fall,
I'm your cushion at the bottom.

Somebody

I need someone to reassure me that I'm not crazy
Someone to rescue me from this insanity
drain the sadness from within me
make things bearable
take the pain away
help me not despise my entirety
listen to my cries
wipe the tears from my eyes
make me not alone
understand me on my own
Someone who doesn't categorize me
doesn't deny my affection or cries
Someone who tries would be nice
Someone to give me the bigger slice
who doesn't need me to hold the knife
Someone who cares
To make me their wife.

thirteen

The Dark Souls

It's not safe here
Walk away
Don't let them touch you
Joyless grins on gray faces
Hopeless eyes bleeding into yours

We are dark souls
We are shadows

Don't let your heart escape
The cage of your ribs
That peppy smile and
Those bright eyes
Light won't survive here
The sun has fallen from the sky
And you are beaming

We don't know light anymore
Stay far away from what goes here
We are the monsters of this world
Shadows of who we were once before

I too was a beautiful ray of light
Thought nothing so bad could ever happen
Everything would turn out
Things will be okay
'We will get through this'
Is what I would say

But I was proven wrong again
And again
The finish line
Always drifting away farther
And farther

Until I gave up
My eyes sunk in
My heart steadied
To a painfully unfeeling
State of indifference
Because nothing mattered
Because nothing ever changed.

Setting the Stage

I began writing long before the age of eleven.
Small things.
I thought I was writing song lyrics
And that my sister, cousin, and myself
would form a band
and become wildly famous.
Like the Cheetah Girls!
Because at that age,
why couldn't we?

Quickly I learned
How silly it was.
To have happy little thoughts.
How delirious of me.

This was growth.
To realize that hope
Is delusional.

Not at six when I thought I
could sing.
Not at seven when I wished my parents
would get back together.

No, I didn't learn this valuable lesson

That hope
Is worthless.

Until maybe eight;
The first time we left
and didn't get far enough.
Or maybe it was nine
The first time that other man
put his hands down my pants.
How I
Pretended I was still asleep
Because I liked
how it felt
And then when it was over
I walked out
Sat on the floor, crisscrossed
With a schoolbook and pen in hand
Pretending to do homework
Just writing my name
Over
And over
Again.
What
Have
I done.
What
Have

I
Done.
And cried
And cried.
And cried.

Having never had a secret
like this
before.

I was only nine.
And I was
a whore.

Maybe that's
the moment
it really
sunk in.

No, life is not
Like the movies.
And nothing good
Ever happens
To us.
And I am not
Beautiful inside
And out.

I am
Wretched.

I am nine.
And I am wretched.

I didn't think about this again
For a long
long time.

Because at that age
how could i?

May 5th, 2024.

Because it took me years
To have the courage
To write this
Out loud.
But I thought
You should know.

Unexpected

I can't breathe, but I don't mind anymore.
It cuts deep, but I don't hurt anymore.
It all mattered to me,
But now I can't seem to find the right mind or
energy
To achieve stability.
So, if you find me staring blankly at a wall while a
knife cuts through me,
Do not misinterpret my blood for bleeding,
Do not misinterpret my tears for weeping,
And do not misinterpret my screams for needing.

Because my body reacts
While my mind does not
And my soul weakens
While *I* am already dead.

Torn

Tear stains and the weather's rains
Both mystify my vision
While you are still oblivious to what occurs under
his supervision

I am always crying, just they are invisible tears
I am always trying, just I never achieve
I have always been dying, just not in a way you can
see

What you don't seem to understand
Is that there is a pain that can only be felt
Not by your hand,
But by the collision of our hearts
And the absence of all realism and shallowness
This is a pain that no two eyes could ever witness
And no whole heart could ever feel

You must be torn as I am
But because you lack the taste of sourness on your
tongue
You could never understand
What it's like to endure the bitter bleeding of cuts
And the loud tearing of hearts

When you have a bullet wound in your chest
And particles of it travel to the rest
Then we may collide our fractured hearts
And make it whole.

Not Today

Trapped
Fingers stuck between the bars
She struggled to reach past them
But they were in her mind
And yet she couldn't control them
The bars were there
But at the same time, they weren't
They were familiar
Used to be there for a long, long time
But they vanished come morning
And everything was to be okay
Things were good
Things were great
Problems so petty
Until one cursed morning
When all of it came crashing down, tumbling
Burning in flames
Washed away with the rain,
She had thought it would be a good day
Lived without the bars for some time
Learned to live without them because
Everything was fine
But one morning
The black started building
Here comes the smell of rust
The feeling of mistrust
Came rushing
Took her down
Left her trembling

But she did not take off running
This she cannot run from
It's not like the other one
Here she is again
Broken down
Skin so thin
It doesn't take much to cut through
Spirits so high
But it never took much
To bring her right back down
She'd tell herself
In wavering whispers
That she'd be okay
It'll be easier
But not today
And she'd scream
In her mind
Why not today?

A Hill Too Steep

To feel like so many people want you to be so
many things
but to be none of them
and feel utterly disturbed
with yourself
and the world
because no one smiles upon all your successes
no one will praise you
they will only glare
and slowly tear
at your self-comfortability
and what you once loved
will be your arch enemy
and what was once okay
will be a hungry insecurity
loving yourself
will become a distant memory
because your goods are never good enough
and your trials too are never enough
your failures set upon a hill too steep
and you often tumble down it
grazing each one on the way down
feeling the way you betrayed yourself
trying to please every one
but yourself

there is a hovering over your shoulder
whispering
taunting

encouraging everything you fear
and withholding everything you hold dear

Tragedy

I am damaged
I am not cured
I am not the perfect little girl
I am damaged from panic attacks
And people turning their backs

I was a lonely child
And I'm a lonely girl
Who is oh so defiant
To adults; otherwise known as giants
I have not fully recovered

This is what I fear
That I will not change
I will not heal
I will just restrain
From living in fear
Or living in the past years

I am a strange teen
Locked up in my worry
Infatuation is my safe haven
When life gets blurry

I am needy
I am frail
I am the box filled with glass
I am the one who scurries from difficulty
The girl who wraps herself in her own arms

Who cuddles the cold at night
Lives in insecurity
Drowns in self-doubt
I am a pitiful character
A spoiled fruit
The unwanted leftovers
In the back of the fridge
I am the small child alone in the corner

I am the result of a tragedy;
a tragedy.

Is it beautiful or is it giving up?

You cursed country
You strange nation
My home

Your shapely streets resemble me
Your scent of breezy night fills me with delight
Your busy streets made me disgruntled
But now I know I love it
Because it's so you
It's so familiar
It's so home

You have so much to offer
But I lived in the dark side
I left; I stepped into the light
So now, dear home
Give me all you can
I've seen your bad
I've been the lonely, broken girl in the crowd
Now show me your bright side
I will take all of you now
I will wear you atop my head
If you'll be my crown

You are my past and my present
I do not resent you anymore
You are my home

I know too many faces here

and had too many heartbreaks here
to not call you my own.

Paws

Invisible paw prints kissed the floor tiles
Unheard meows floating in the air
Claw marks are fading
Stray fur will be washed away

She was the warmth
She was home
She was what made me feel not so alone
No one understood
No one saw her the way I did
No one understood her the way I did

Taken away
She was taken away
The house feels different
It's cold. It's impersonal
It's not home
I'm all alone

Sometimes I forget that she's gone
And I turn to look at her
Sometimes I hear her
Sometimes I even see her
But it's never her
She's not here
And it hurts so bad
When I remind myself that

And it all comes crashing down

And it hurts so bad
Because in that tiny moment
When I forgot, and thought she was there
I felt okay
And then I remember
And just like that
It's taken away
I'm not okay

Daddy!

He wasn't even trying
her eyes are fighting the dullness
Daddy broke the medicine

Her breathing heavy
she saw Daddy fighting Mom again and wishes
this life wasn't hers
the light gone from her eyes
she realized Daddy doesn't love Mom
That Daddy doesn't love her either
a sag of darkness under her eyes
she was hurting all over, sobbing
Hated her life
Daddy was the first man to break her heart

Is she still trying to get out?
No, she gave up on that
You have your whole life ahead of you!
Maybe you do, but I don't
Daddy broke his promises every time so she
learned
Early on
That nothing ever happens

Daddy didn't love her so neither did she
and maybe she fears that she'll be just like Daddy
Or maybe he messed her up so good in the head
that she doesn't
know herself or

ginger h. goodall

how to unravel the mess

fourteen

ginger h. goodall

A Chapter for My Unconditional Mother

Mother and Daughter

Since conceived
I have been surrounded by your lovely warmth
In a place so cold
I was a lonely something-year-old
But one look into your eyes
I knew everything would be alright
Maybe if I held onto your hand tight enough
If I looked into your eyes long enough
It would be okay

It was hard
The waves crashed and pulled me away
I changed a lot
But to you, I know I'm always the same

I find myself closer to you everyday
When the rain falls, you're my shelter
And knowing you're near when the night comes
I sleep better
You smile and the sun comes out to play
You're that bit of reality and that bit of okay
You're funny and smiley
Smart and feisty

I know that you love me not just because you have
to.
Because I have told you things
That would turn anyone away
No, you love me because

You choose to.

Despite
Everything.

December 9ᵗʰ, 2016.

All She Ever Wants Is a Cup of Joe

And so I know I've said this before
But I'm sorry for not making enough coffees for
you
Because you deserve them all

You wake in the mornings for us
Early as can be
And head to work
A job you never asked for
Just for us
All you ever wanted
A stay-at-home mom
But by the time you get back
You're exhausted
I know

Meanwhile I drink my hot cup of tea
And I don't have it in me to fetch you a coffee
I thought it was the parent's role to say "no"
But I'm afraid I've taken the job
The word leaves my lips more often than not

And I want you to have everything
Because you have given me everything
And leave yourself nothing
All the time.
Find & Seek on the Screen
You're sleeping right now
I can hear your snoring from the end of the hall

The moments we just shared
Are the ones I cherish above all
When we lay side by side on our stomachs
Sing silly songs
While we play old computer games
And laugh over the smallest of things
Curve our lips and curl our noses
Into those goofy faces
Just for fun

It's early in the morning
The sun shone through the balcony
But *you* lit up the room
What with your contagious laugh
And humorous attitude

I wish I could wake you in an hour
With a forest of trees
And maybe some flowers
And if I could make you a garden
I would grow it just beneath your nose
And you would smell rose
And heather
And the greenest of grass
I know how much you miss it all

I wish I could wake you up every morning
With a big, warm mug of freshly brewed coffee and
milk
And an omelet to go with that fine drink

The beautiful symphony of your mother's fingers
stroking a piano
Because I know you get homesick

And the list goes on
And on
Because you deserve so much
And you haven't been given enough
I can't make up for it now
But I will keep trying.

He Took the Best Years of Your Life

You smile through the tears
Even though you gave up the best of your years
I want you to know
I acknowledge your pain
I see the flood of emotions seeping through the
cracks
Of your big brick wall
Each brick another heartbreak
Each brick another sacrifice you make
And I know you try so hard to hide it all
But you're lonely most nights
And tired from all the countless fights
I *know* you're hurting
And I just want you to know
I feel every ache that follows the pump of your
heart
I know you laugh through it all
I know you try not to think about it
Or do things that might trigger it
I know what you've been through
I know what you're going through
And I can't thank you enough
Going through all that
For us

Growing up
Seeing what my father did to you.
You always told me
"I'd do it again to get you."
"I'd do it a hundred times."
And I *know*
You mean it.

Moms Are Allowed to Have Bad Days

Don't feel ashamed of being in a bad place
Or having a bad day

Life throws you curve-balls and you whack them
with a bat
Attacks don't faze you
They might graze you

You come out strong
Because you know where you belong and where
you came from
I know you miss that farm you grew up on
But you hold on
Your grip never falters

There are so many things that are temporary to me
But your love is the only thing that cannot be
altered
Our bond is made up of slow games and old T.V.
shows
Virtual Villagers and Gilligan's Island.

You are my flashlight when the candle burns out
You are my helmet
The thing that keeps me from plummeting into
disaster
You are the constant
The humor and the strive
You are the only mother of mine

I want you to sleep undisturbed
In a cushion of serene dreams
I want you to laugh at silly things
I want your mouth turned up in a smile

This feeling you have will only last for a while
Just remember the things you tell me
And you'll be fine
You always face it and make it
Why would that change now?
You're positively positive
Quirky all the way
That's what will get you through

Strut your strut
And shake your butt
Because... well, just because.
That'd be funny.

You Have the Right to Grow Too

I settled in your womb so no wonder I was late
I surely didn't want to leave your homey embrace
You put me into this world
And did all you could to shield me
It's not your fault
I was destined to be messed up
It's not your fault
You were just trying to survive
Can't protect us from everything all at once
I know that you were just
Trying to find love
I know that you were just
Hurting
I know that you were
Trying
Mom
I know you are
Always
Trying

You Don't Hear It Enough

Sleeping soundly – literally; you snore
You're the epitome of *home*
Dealt a set of cards that really weren't pleasant at
all
You've played them well
Considering the cards were bad as hell
You are the friendliest person I know
Find hilarity and bemusement in the worst
And you never look down on anyone or anything –
except perhaps your feet

You work day and night
Even after all these years, you've still got fight
You always provide and you are my most reliable
guide
You teach me well even though I don't always
abide
You're one of those fascinating people; the ones
who are always so happy
But just beneath the surface they hide
And I know most days are difficult for you

I know I don't show you enough
Or tell you enough
And that's why I'm writing this
Solely out of adoration
Because it often slips my tongue
So I'll try to catch it here.

ginger h. goodall

Toot

I don't wish to have been born into a different
family
Even though ours isn't perfect or ordinary
Even though ours isn't complete
We have struggled to live
We have struggled to eat
I wouldn't trade it for another mother I would
sooner starve by your side
You live off crumbs
In more ways than one
You are always
Sacrificing
For us.

We don't have much money
It always goes.
But you are rich with talent and charming tales
So enrich me, please
Tell me all your stories
Even the ones you've told for years
Tell me again, teach me; I'm all ears
Tell us about your far away loved ones
Across deep seas
And those antics you were up to
Those days when you were young
Before you lost everything

You are a bundle of honesty dipped in ice tea
You are positively charming and lovely

You're all that a mother can and should be
With a dash of *you*, and a poof as well
You taught us about
Important things
Like beans
The magical fruit
The more you eat
The more you

These Days

You've soothed rough years with smiles through
the tears
And you've extracted countless laughs that made
my bad days just a little bit less
I love playing those timeless games
Laying on our stomachs and watching The Hunger
Games

I've yearned for a plane
To find *home*
From where *you* came
Where everyone speaks our language
And I can show my cleavage and my ankles
And we can be free

But I realize the travel would be no greater gain
Than when I'm sat here beside you
Because those adventures can be made later
These moments are the ones I can never get again.

- I will look back on

December 17ᵗʰ, 2020.

I Propose a Toast

may the moments last
don't look away when you fill your glass
before you know it, everything's passed
you'll look back and ask where it's at
may the treasure remain forever in your grip
beware, don't loosen, you might just lose it
and miss the feeling in the palm of your hand
may you not dwell over treachery
or break endlessly... like me
may you live steadily, not *be* chaotically like me
i don't ask of you to be heavenly
angelic, or sweet like a melody
just don't be melancholy... like me
learn that the sweetness may be drenched in bitter
but that's the fun of digging deeper
don't lose yourself on the way there
on the path to where you want to be
when you're still not sure who you are
because then you've got nothing to go by, and
nothing to rely on
you'll be nothing but a shell
and build yourself back up based on memory of
being well
and may you not fear that heart-breaking theory
or that gut-wrenching misery
may you live, love, have hope and faith; all of the
above... whole-heartedly
don't ever *be* unsurely like me
don't ever worry about what the future may hold

because it will never be what it's meant to
unless you just let it be
don't wait for it, whatever you're waiting for
to put a smile on your face
"tell me when it's beautiful"
if you're waiting for that, you might as well sit back
because it's never, ever going to be like that
and you'll look back thinking of the things you
could've done instead
of waiting around
for a wish, a sign, a sound,
telling you what you want can and will be found
don't be afraid of what might be
because if you do, it may turn out to be something
very
much like me

One of Them is Not Like the Others

Disappear into the crowd
It won't matter, you weren't going to make anyone
proud
Dissipate among them if you don't become them
Individuality lost its quality
I feel like fleeing from everyone
And going missing
With no one's notice
I'm just being honest.
Tell me where I went wrong
By being me or being myself?
By trying hard or trying my best?
When will these people give it a rest?

I'm not...
I'm not like the rest
I am strange and cowardly
I'm me, is that faulty?
Let your judgment rain down on me
Weigh me down until I'm down on the ground
Pressure me and point me out
Why don't you be more like us?
One of them is not like the others
One of them is not like the others
One of them is not like the others
But why do we have to be one?
I knew I wasn't going to last,
I am a fool to think I could fit in their normality.

Apples

I'm not so foolish to believe in a fine family tree
The apples are bruised
The children are abused
We are the children of selfish men
We are made up of them

We are the failures and trials
Of our unapologetic fathers
We are the broken hearted
The once open hearted
We are the ones who float on cigarette smoke
Children of the damned
We are the uproar
The anti-familiarity
The ones who run away
We are the children who played differently
The ones who fill their abyss with bad habits
Promise themselves they'll be okay a sooner day
We are the defiled innocence in an unjust
household
The damaged without antidote
We are the fragile and the calloused
The strength of the weak
The faithful and the lost
Angels fallen in ash and dust
Strangers among us.

S-S-Society

we're all just trying to fit into our old jeans
we're all looking at the stretch marks,
cutting ourselves with dreams
of who we want to be
trying to scrub ourselves clean after a night with a
man
because women are shut down
for just fooling around
we're all just trying to sip our tea in peace
without the call or whistle
or the stare at our asses
we're just trying to hold on to our glasses
get through the classes
and have some blackstrap molasses
men can turn to many things in times of desire
but we have to cross our legs
and fight men off our beds
we're just girls turning into women in pearls
cover yourself and don't offer yourself
half of humanity wants what you have
but it's not ladylike
behave
your collar's too low
and your smile is suggestive
shut your face
close your legs
all that's left is your open heart
no wonder women hurt so much
there is no gateway to our hearts

but our hearts are the gateway
to what men want
maybe that's why
we lock ourselves up.

realizing the background state of mind

i am in pain
i have always been in pain
i always will be in pain
because when there is nothing wrong with my life
there is something wrong with me
and so everywhere i look
every time i turn around
something is wrong
and it seems to dim the *right* to a subtle *okay*
so that everything becomes *fine*
and i am mostly numb
screeching in the background
happiness was briefly found
but lost
when knowledge was gained
the more you know
the less you have
because at the end of every cycle,
every connected sequence of events and life's
questions,
there is a dark pit in which everything ultimately
falls into.
i can be happy
when i belittle myself
and shut off the part of me that became a big girl
mute certain thoughts and beckon the child in me
to play
sometimes i feel as though i am in a classroom
taking an exam

and the clock is hung on the wall in front of me
i fret, and i sweat
as my time tick tocks its way between my fingers,
every second precious
and gone too fast
sometimes, everything seems to be pointless; as it
all comes to an end
in the waiting room
waiting for our names to be called
but it won't bring good news
because who knows what comes next
who knows if there really is a heaven
or a hell
all the questions with no answers...
they make me afraid
so scared that i can't take two steps without a
shake
i should have been more careful with myself from
the start
i put band-aids on cuts and ice on my bruises
but i let my mind fall and wander into darkened
creases
it's not a break for which you can glue up the
pieces
it's something lost
a search that could last a lifetime
often i just think it's the poet in me
that led me to see
just how dreary a life can be
if i had not questioned
the birds or the trees

73

i would not have questioned
God or peace
and i would have known for myself
what peace may be
because then my mind and my heart
would be at ease

The Lonely Ones

the lonely ones have been calling
upon someone to call them darling
of a silhouette drawn in ink
wrapped in a rugged physique
on the pages that they read
of the man in their dreams
a recollection of the author's masterpiece
details inscribed in their minds
of their sharp collar bones
and their divine eyes
they do not have plans
only dreams... of a man
but they call in cries
feel at loss without this man of lies
he is a product of imagination
a pattern of the alphabet
without the man they see only through text on
these pages
they convince themselves that they are empty
because they are blinded by what the main
character needs
they see
they see
they see this man in their dreams
and they find themselves lonely
they fall falsely
delve deeply
into the last ones they'd need
because they share some similarity

with the man on their bookshelf
the silhouette in their minds
the man in their dreams

the lonely ones spread their arms
towards one who resembles him
the books tell them that they are empty
spending their lives just searching
for the one...
that they do not have time to heal
to discover who they are
until their time has come
they race too quickly
for a life out of reach
that they give their love to one unworthy

oh... they forget to love themselves
they get lonely without someone else
that they waste themselves
in imposters
they waste their breath on whispered nothings
fading out of existence
like the lovers
they are loving

at 14, I thought I was in love

He used words in the English language
That were beautiful
On their own
And all too cheesy
Put together

Sentences I thought
Repulsive
Prior to the event of him
Yet they made my heart melt
Into honey
On his tongue
If only
He liked honey
Half as much
As he liked beer

I've tasted both
And unless it's the fog
Of the mind
That you want
Unless it's the illusion of being awake
That you can't live without
Then you should have found
Paradise
In the subtlety of me

Alcohol wears off
And when your eyes peel open the next morning

So bland one would think you were mourning
But I never would have faded
My love would have never worn away

- *Don't* Talk to Strangers!

Let's begin at the end

i'll wait
and when 12 p.m. comes around again
i hold my breath
to see your name pop up on my screen
a refreshing change
to how your name flashes bright
like New York's neon signs
in my head
all damn night
keeping me up
holding my heart tight
and when it has passed
though i haven't seen your face
my heart drops in my ribcage
because your distance from me hasn't changed
and you won't answer
my incoming calls
no you don't
you don't answer
at all
if i was there
i'd be knocking at your door
but all i can do here, now
is knock on your heart
and wait

by the gates of your ribcage
waiting
for you to open them
open the floodgates

2:54 a.m.
someday *in June of 2017.*

He was much older

if only you asked for what i gave
if i didn't spill my heart into the screen
the glass couldn't keep me from loving you
but maybe there was a bad connection that day
because it didn't seem to reach you
you didn't see me spill it through the barrier

if only we had less time between us
less land between us
if only you gave it a chance
if you gave me a call
we'd fix it all

if only i could move on
if i could ship it by mail
leave my heart at your doorstep
you could stomp on it
or you could open the door
anything
i just want more

i miss your calls
i miss your smile
i miss seeing you on my desk
in my computer screen

i thought this was love

August 13th, 2017.
but really i just
missed my chance
to have somebody
anybody

So he never called me sober

you never deserved all the poems I wrote about
you
so I will condense them here because you are
really
not a chapter, no, not even just.

i wish i was drunk too
i wish i couldn't remember

you deleted me
turned me right back into a stranger again
it only took a click to break my heart

wouldn't it just be nice
if i could forget you
like you forgot me
if i could click you away
like you did with me

you drown your sorrows in alcohol
i would too if i could
but instead i drowned in myself
between lyrics i can't hear
and melodies i feel

i thought it was safe to fall
thought you weren't like them all
but now you're just another man who put me
down

and let me fall to crash into the ground

-    men always hurt me
                August 14th to September 9th, 2017.

Silly, Stupid Girl

you walked away in the middle of a song

i cried alone
i cried in the shower
i cried at night
i cried at the random hour
i cried in my pillow
i cried in a dog's fur
it wasn't even my dog
but my tears
they don't collide
with your heart
they just fall back onto mine
and start over

this is so unhealthy for me
to be thinking of you still
you just ran away
through coward's silence
and the click of a button
you broke me down
i melted in my gown
and i...
i'll never be the same
i'm not the same girl again
i don't want love
i don't want anyone in my heart
there already wasn't enough space for me in there
it should just be me

i already hurt myself enough
i don't need another man to tear me down
every man i've known

has been a liar on their throne in my heart
took a torch to my love
every man i've ever known
took me down
down
why should i
let another man
in my life
in my heart
to tear me down again?

fuck the world
and fuck its men
i don't need your empty promises...
believed you once
believed you twice
believed you all
gave you everything
gained nothing true
gained only empty words through you
all the drunken promises
the confessions you later called untrue
i love you
i love you
i thought that you loved me too
maybe that was the problem
i liked to believe that you weren't running from me

you were running from the love you felt for me
but this is me we're talking about
and men love to throw my heart around
and i tend to be naive

i really thought that you loved me.
gosh, how stupid am i
to cry over this guy
i met online
how stupid am i
to give my heart away
to some guy on my screen

who gave me drunken sugar
sweet words laced with bitter alcohol
September 10th, 2017.
Because you couldn't justify
Saying those things to me sober
No, because
I was fourteen
And you were too much older
You never meant a word you said
And you shouldn't have

But I was just a little girl
Looking for The Man on Her Bookshelf
Wasting myself
In imposters
Wasting away
On whispered nothings
That faded out of existence

Just like the lover
She thought
She was loving.

Many years later

Tree House Queens

Behind the trampoline
We were Tree House Queens
Spoiled lemonade was our whiskey
And animals were our envy
Fit into the shelves and slide
Through the doors
Hide and seek
The night is yours

Fight over Totally Spies
Dream of blue-eyed guys
Pray wishes but don't bet on their fruition
Your wish is God's command
But that is a sweet, sweet lie
Your fevered nights of escape and blazing lights
Show you were a troublesome one
And angelic somehow
Shows you prayed but no one came
You are not the one to blame
Wooden spoons and a kick to the face
Donkey manure handed to you on life's copper
plate
Say silly lies and let me believe
You can channel a celebrity through your mind
Play with the lights and creep under the covers
Speak to me now about the monsterly others
We were children of separate age
And separate fathers
But our mother joined us

89

And life challenged us
Let there be no stronger duo than two sisters
Back-to-back
Although we pulled each other's hair
And tattletaled to our mother
Give us a mutual enemy
And watch them suffer.

- *Sisterhood*

Lost

I had just met her two seconds before
She looked through my sketchbook
Then she looked through my eyes
And asked me if I had lost someone
My immediate response was 'no'
Because no one of my family or friends had died
But then I thought
Maybe she could see
That I lost my mother to her work
And I lost my sister to her depression
And my father to his narcissism
Or maybe
She could see the countless times
I had lost myself
To my school
To my anxiety
To my insanity
Could she see all that through the strokes of my
paintbrush?
Or perhaps she could tell
That I was indeed lost
... Maybe I think too much
That's more than enough.

silent film

hurt quietly
burn silently
cry solemnly

shut your heart,
your blood is staining their clean white clothes

stop crying,
your tears are drenching their ignorance
and your pain
is much too painful for them to bear

your hurt is an inconvenience
shut up
you're wreaking havoc
they're too busy to acknowledge you're tearing
apart
the flood of your emotions is wetting their dry
hearts

People Like Us

People like us
Have to feign happiness
In order to feel it

We are not happy
Though we experience
Some form of it
To keep ourselves going

People in my life
Are like water
And I retain them
Like a flask
But what's the point
Of gaining these droplets
When they will all leave me
Leaving holes behind
Springing leaks in my being
And my mind

-   anxiety, weak of the mind

November of 2017

ginger h. goodall

fifteen

Quiet the Mind

And I'm afraid
that I'll never be happy,
Because the voices inside
don't usually listen to me

3:45 p.m.
December 31st, 2017.

Emotional

No song can speak of how I feel
Something longed for
Is something unreal

And am I strange
To be saddened
By sadness itself?

I am weathered
My sanity is fleeting
I don't often feel strong
In fact, it's almost never at all

My emotions carry me around
Like an ocean wave amidst dry land
My hair is bleached, lightened
But I am still tainted
Tarnished

I am left confused
On a gloomy day
On a clear day
I am confused
My tear ducts are used
For every emotional sway
My hormones grab a hold of me
Roughly
These days

I am sorry
I am sorry
For what, I can't say
Because these days it's for everything

That's my everything everything
Sometimes

9:21 p.m.
February 15th, 2018.

struggles of uniquity

I want to say a million things
But you will not comprehend
So I keep my mouth shut
While I swallow the bile and vomit
Or regurgitate it into my hand
Because you
You will not understand from my tellings
When I myself cannot fathom it
So ask me why
There is a silence
At the lunch table
And ask me
What
Is troubling me

February of 2018.

The Things I Take with Me

Mom.
You may not have been able to teach me to play
piano
Or how to sew a dress
But you taught me something else
Something some people never realize
Never are familiar with
Not from their mothers or fathers
At least, not around here.
You taught me unconditional love
What it feels like
To receive it
To give it
And what it looks like
So I can know it when I see it

You taught me
You taught me
You taught me things
Most valuable
Like how to be strong enough
To hold on
How to make my mind adapt
To what's going on
And I'm just grateful
That I'm not one of those people

Who never learn to appreciate
Especially their mothers
But sometimes I think
I love you too much

     –   your best has always been enough for me

March 10th, 2018.

God's Will

after a year or more of trying to do what's best for
me
and everyone i value
after so many desperate and determined tries
i've decided that life is not my decision
my life has never been and is not in my hands
i can't make my own history
i can't choose my future
because i have no control over where the wind
blows
so i decided to stop holding onto the lamp pole
and let the wind take me where it may
because as they say
it's God's will
and God's will and mine don't seem to agree
who do you think wins the argument, though?
i never stood a chance

March 17th, 2018.

silly me, why so dramatic over the same old tree?

I am wilting
Wilting
Beneath expectancy
I am wailing
I'm wailing
In open seas
It's taking over
Over
Over me
I am falling
Falling
Down under me
I am crying crying
To fill your wells
Your water
Refreshing
Can't you taste the salt
I am torn
I am tearing
Apart
Under this tree
Fruits falling
All over me
I am buried
Buried
Beneath
Roots are wrapping
They're wrapping
All around me

I am strangled
Untangle me
Trying to please
Every fruit in the tree
I am terrified
Of failing
I am troubling
I'm troubling me
So don't punish me
Don't bother
I've already begun
And it hurts already
You needn't add
Please someone save me
I am drying up and falling ill
I am trying to please you
I am trying to tame myself
To calm myself
And tend to a grandmother
Give me a break
I am trying
With everything
But I cannot perfect everything
I am trying my best
I'm sorry if it's not good enough for you
But you're giving me anxiety
That's more than enough punishment from the
inside
Just please
Give me a break
I'm an earthquake

When I get that mental shake
Don't push me over the edge
I'm not strong enough to arise unchanged
And you know how fear changes me
How I fear change
Just please
Give me peace
And joy
Don't hurtle me
When I walk back through the door
I don't know what to do anymore
I'm done
I'm a broken door
But that won't stop people from slamming me

April of 2018.

Day-To-Day

Differences between you and I
One too many breakdowns
One too many meltdowns
Unshared
I was unprepared
Too many lies
Spewed to form my nest
While you were at rest
In a comfortable bed
Still we both stream red

Difference is
You're not too scared
To live
And find out what comes next
No, because you are strong
In your muscles on your arm
And the sponge in your head

Give me something of yours
That energy
That stability
Give me your calm
Give me some of the build
That holds you together
Please
Because I seem to have lost mine

Tell me your secret

I promise I won't keep it
I'll use it
And see if it will fix me
But my Momma tells me
The only solution
Is within
I tell her
Ma, it's hard
To control my brain
I'd rather take a pill
To make it go away
But she said my name
And told me
That's how people decay

So tell me your secret
Because I didn't see you take any pills today

Functionality
Is lost with me
Tell me how
To sleep soundly
And live loudly
Somebody explain to me
How you might know what I know
But be so alive
Why are you not reacting like me?
I wish I could ask somebody
The people around me
But they don't know
They won't understand

Because I am not
And never was
Anything like them

April 24th, 2018.

ginger h. goodall

Birdie & Tree

The dead tree's sharp bark
Pricked the bird's feet
So the birdie flew away
Without a moment's delay

Leaves fallen to the roots
This tree once was beautiful
But now it can't withstand a birdie
Perched on its branch
It can't keep a birdie at all
Because somehow the weight of this little bird
Feels like an avalanche

The Day After Rain

I don't particularly like rainy days,
having always been sheltered from them
But I quite like the aftermath.
There's always been something special
about the following couple of days...
It's like the city has been bathed;
The trees wiped from dust
and the streets mopped.
And boy, does this filthy city
need a wash.

A B C's

Sorry I'm dropping the A's into B's
But I'm just trying to be a functioning human now
So let me do as I please
Lest I fall under my own knees
You won't be able to lift me up and bend me back
into shape
Let my grades fall apart so my mind may be at
ease
I would beg for a cure
But I've never gotten what I wanted before
And I don't expect things to change, not anymore

Again I'm sorry for letting my A's drop to B's
And they'll probably drop to C's
Let's just hope I discover sanity
Before the end of the alphabet finds me

strange relationships

It was the first day that determined everything
How we meet
Sets up how we speak

But don't you worry
I have a crush on everyone once
It'll pass
You'll get sick of me
And I hope I'll turn around
Before you turn me away

    -   yes, another crush. another distraction.

11:11 a.m.
July 3rd, 2018.

relocation

I wonder if the air tastes different out there
Here it may be more polluted
But I know I'm used to it
Maybe 'clean' is lacking to me
Maybe 'ideal' isn't so ideal to me
Or maybe I'm just lonely
So I want my family homely
I know every other face
It's familiar
It's what I know
And it has grown on me
Absorbed into me
Added into my taste

pivotal moments

Like that time when I was about nine
I spun and spun
In circles
Until my head hurt
And my stomach ached
And I felt like my life's food consumption
Was about to leave through my mouth
That was the last time
I ever spun

Hey

'Hey'
That's all it takes
To make me think better
Instead of
Of my mistakes

F

Oh do I regret it now
But I tried, Auntie
I tried to get you those A's
But my grades burned to a blaze
When my calm had escaped

But I know my potential
I know what I can do
Next time I'll bring back letters that bring pride
onto you.

what if?

Home
You have to take the idea with you
But make it empty
Because everything that makes your home home
Should not be temporary
Or not within your hold
Because people leave
And old things mold
You have to fill the concept of home
Wherever you go
Don't hold on to things and people
That you'll have to let go
But who am I to give that advice
Do as I say not as I do
Well, I've held on to everything temporary in my
life
And I can't let go
I'd still cry and try to reach them
From a ten-foot pole
I hold on
I clutch them all to my heart
Before all else
So that when they're gone
Or I have to say I'm moving on
I will be broken
I will be gone
I'm trying to loosen my grip
Until I can let go
But I can't

I fall off my bike
Without them at my hold
Why do people have to grow old
Why do things have to change
How much strength do I have to gain
Before I'm rid of the pain
Of what happened
Of what goes on
Of what's to come
I should be young
I should be living it up
But I feel like I'm chasing life in circles
It's an obstacle course
And behind me
I'm chasing myself with a knife
How am I ever to be a wife
I cannot be anything right
I am everything done abnormally
I am a deformity
Because of what this life had in hold for me
I slip in and out
Of a pool
I cannot swim
But there is life underwater
That makes the drowning a little sweeter
Sometimes
I can't tell
If I'm above ground
Or I'm still swallowing sea water
And that's when people dislike me
Because I am strange

I am easily troubled
And I don't do what I'm told

What IF
What I Fear
Life in itself,
My dear.

Now tell me
What I can do about it.

sixteen

Not A Sixteen Queen

Sixteen years old
not much has changed
except now I feel I'm
getting old
My hair is growing out
The guy I like won't take me out
I eat too much take-out
These days.
Didn't do nothing to celebrate
Everything always comes late
It didn't bring me to hate
It's just my inevitable fate
These days
are a tad
too cold.
I wanted
to do something
incredible.
I wanted to
make something
of myself.
I wanted
to be
credible.
But lately I've been
mediocre.
I even wore a
choker.
When am I

going back
to being
original?

January 1ˢᵗ, 2019.

Settling

Now I know why
Women settle for less
It's because they found the guy
The nice one in a vest
The kind of guy she deserved
But he thought he deserved
Better
So she thought she deserved
Worse
And so she settled

January 15th, 2019.

Mother & Daughter

When I fucked up
You said it was okay
And so when you fucked up
I said it was okay
We know it's not
We know we're wrong
But this is how we grow
This is how we move on

January 29th, 2019.

Lust & Intellect

Desirable
I want to be wanted
For my mind
That's the gold
For my body
That's more common
So I'm told
But I don't mind so much
Anymore
If that's all I can get
Then I'll take some of it
If I can't win them over with my words
My language
My intellect
Then I'll reel them in with my body
I'll tell them dirty words
I'll be naughty
I'll be good
And you'll just wish I was in your bed
But you'll have to read me instead

- i could never go through with it

Father's Tantrums

Is it forbidden
For you to love me
Will you be bitten
If you were to show me
One drop of fatherly
Am I so
Unwelcome in your heart
Why is it so
Difficult for you
To give it up
And give me what
I deserve
Am I so worthless
Are you that short of a nerve
You leave me in dire situations
They call for extreme circumstances
I'm not sure what's going to happen
But what I do know
Is that it's all on you,
Dad.

Acknowledgement

Things are good
Things are great
I try hard to appreciate
I don't always show it
I sometimes forget it
And find reasons to complain
But things are so much better now
Than they were before we left him
For good this time
Things turn bad
And I go sad
It's so easy for me to stay angry
But it feels safer
It sort of makes me glad
In a way
Because familiarity is so comfortable
It makes me more humble
And so towards sadness I more-so gravitate
Things are wonderful
Things are just lovely
I'm not lonely in most ways but one
I try not to focus on it but I'm afraid I've become
One of those people who need romance as if
sucking on their thumb
I don't need a man
But boy do I want one
Things get stressful
I get tired
But compared to before

It's way, way mild
I try to remind myself
Of previous toil
So that I will not just put those memories on a
shelf
I will use them to realize that life is better now
Things depress me
Things impress me
Unfortunately they are
Usually one and the same
Which makes it much harder
For me to stay sane

January 21st*, 2019.*

New Boy

Some boy at school
Means nothing to me
But he called me pretty
And that gave me glee
He was to choose
Between me or her
She has clear skin
A small nose
And soft wavy hair

He chose her.

Of course
He chose her.

I Would Rather Do This

I don't know if you'll notice
I don't know if you'll care
But tonight I wasn't there
This is me letting go.
You were anything but an investment.

    –   the nice guy in the vest

Scripted

Guys aren't like that though
They don't say the right things
Or come at the right time
They don't call when you want them
Or show up when you need them.
They're disappointment after disappointment
Wrapped in magnetic wrapping paper
And tied with a pretty bow

Youth Gathered and Contained

In this province there are only two places
Where I can meet peers with more familiar faces
But they lack the warmth I crave
They don't act the way I behave
And they seem empty of any wants at all
They are obedient and child-like
Although we should by now have grown
No traces of sarcasm
Not one groan
A room full of teenagers
But not one of them knows
What it's like
To live the life of a teen
To be selfish
Sexual
And sometimes mean.
It's like the guys
Have no dicks
And the girls
Have no wits
I don't know how they can think like this
The guys take the right side
We girls sit to the left
I want to reach out
But they might judge me to death
No flirting
No dates
No hand-touching
No, not one trace.

In this community we must grow with grace
I know, I know
But God wants us to live
The lives that he gave us
We are no nuns nor monks
So why treat us as such
We are meant to be brave
Idiots at times
This is our time to make mistakes
To have fun
And be a disgrace
We should do this all now
Lest it overflow and pour out
If you don't let it
Watch it fester and pester
You until it erupts from your mouth
Palms will make their way
Where they have not been
The human mind is curious
And our hands follow its path
On the road to exploration
Where everything must be had
They will not all be so innocent
When they leave your embrace
I know it is meant as love
But it sure feels like a cage

I will leave these angels to your holy games
I will feed my hunger
While you starve them insane
Then when I have reached my calm
They will run loose and not know what they've
done
I'll say I told you so
Shouldn't you have let them
Have their fun
Now look around you
One's numb and one's lost
The first unaware of what they missed out on
The second all too knowing
And in search but in conflict
With themselves and with God
Because they were told this was wrong
For heaven's sake
A little fun
Will harm no one
If life is always so bitter
Then it would be a sour existence for everyone

January 25ᵗʰ, 2019.

Our First and Only Date

I had an awful
Wonderful dream
It was you
And I was in your lap
And you were holding me.

    –   that nice guy in the vest

Joining In on The Fun

We give our selves up
Because he claims us to love
We spread our legs
In belief that he cares
Then he breaks our damn hearts
Because he thinks we have spares
Well guess what
I'm done
With these games
They're no fun
For us!
I'll join them
Won't toy them like
They did to us
I simply want to spread my
Legs just for the fun
I don't want love
Don't want to hear it
Not once
Honey, I know,
It's hard to believe it
But sometimes girls really do
Just want to have fun

One Hundred and Thirty Thousand Pound Signature

Fatherly Father
The Man Who Couldn't Bother
to write down his name
rid my sister of this frame
that's been squeezing her down
until she hides underground
for fear that they'll take her
cuff her and throw her
or send her away
My sister's not ready.
Her life would decay.
You'd better make way
for my wrath on that day
if I ever have to face
another tragedy in her fate

11 a.m.
February 10th, 2019.

I Am the Reason. I Am the Faulty One.

If there's one thing that hide and seek has taught
me
It's how to hide
Because I am never the seeker
Never so inclined
For any one or thing to find
I hide from most things
But not the kind you expect
I hide not from despair or regret
I hide from joy and change
Exhilaration even if nice
I hide from difficulty
I don't try
But I attempt to try...
The people around me
They're telling me things
That these things are all in my head
That I can make it if I please
That I have no such reason to sit in my place and
wheeze
They're right in one way of two
It is all in my head
But it is more than enough reason
To sit still
Right here
And wheeze
Instead I should
Weave
My future

With delicacy and gentle care
But I am staring wide-eyed, mouth agape
Looking at others' masterpieces
Carpets and quilts that could amaze at the least
And hundreds of ways
To weave something akin to that piece
But I do not want to search for the thread
Prick my finger so many times on the needle
Make so many stiches
So many wrong moves
When I already feel like my whole mind
Is made up of glitches
It is all in my head
But where else do I put it?

How Ironic. That My Face Cannot Show That Which Occurs Most Often

Hard face?
Angry expression?
I thought there was no question
Tears are festering
Emotions welling up
Both simultaneously threatening to fall
And yet you see nothing of this
You don't see any of it at all
I am torn in the sense that
I have been tearing myself apart.
I've been feeling real bad
The thoughts whirling around my head are too sad
I'm trying to hold it together
I tell you I can't talk
But you take it the wrong way
Suddenly I am in the wrong
And I have been misplaced
You want to send me back home
Now I can't stand to look at your face
Home was only home because you were there
Now there is no such homely place
I know now that you drew realistic conclusions
I just thought you knew me better
I thought you understood
I never thought you would react the way you did
Say the things you did
Suddenly the negativity that had been building up
when we left the room

It was nothing
Incomparable to the likeness of you

When Not Even You Can Handle Me

When you act as though my pain
Is too much for you to bare
That is when it exceeds excruciating

I Can't Watch Sad Movies

A sad film
It starts
The opening of doors that
Halt
The floods
Suddenly everything
Has sad undertones
And it begins to pour
Bitterness on my whole little world

A Favor

Talking to you now just makes me feel depressed
I should give it a fucking rest
You have no interest
Why am I so hooked
On your every word
They're all meaningless
They're all no good
Your name is a
Lie.
I don't know how
that applies
But your name is
a lie.

- crushing is exhausting

In-Between

It's tiring
To lay down...
To sit up
My body hurts
To close my eyes
To keep them wide
They ache
To talk
To be quiet
They don't ask twice
They wouldn't understand anyway
To go out
To stay in
To cancel plans with friends
To go socialize with them
I'm just too tired
For the storyline
The plot
I'm too impatient
Because I've already seen
What comes next
And what that means

March 14th, 2019.

The Wait

I'm just waiting
Either for this to blow over and
Life to be smoother
Or for doom to settle
As people do mettle
In my life like it's not mine
End my strife, no they wouldn't be so kind
I just don't want my tragedies to be another's
demise

March 15th, 2019.

Zzz...

Force me to sleep
I want to fall asleep now
Nothing to amuse me no more hits to go bruise me
just use me
I want sleep to consume me for the night I'm just
Z's
Don't make me say please. I just want a sudden
short sleep

Sorry

I'm sorry
I'm sorry
I'm sorry
For what?

For opening my mouth
And for keeping it shut

March 16th, 2019.

Temptations

Turning you on
It was an accident
But boy do I want
To do that again

You're still my friend
But I can't just pretend
Like you weren't something
Nice to look at first

The thought of being with you just
Makes me want to burst
Not in the sense of love
Ew, no. Yuck.
I mean it in the sense of lust.

Absentminded

Fantasies, oh fantasies
They are making a whore of me

So here's the idea of it
If we do it under the covers
It'll never be known to others

Say It

Sometimes when we ask a question
It's not to know the answer
But to hear the answer being said
I myself
Am guilty of this

Homequake

One wants to kill herself
The other wants to leave
And here I am
Stuck in the very between

Trying to find compromise
Trying to play nice
Every word I speak
Causes another uprise

I know I spent the last four days in bed
Shutting everyone out
But I didn't mean to push you away
I was just busy malfunctioning
I don't know what happened
Or why it struck me silent and aching for sleep
A nothingness
I crawled into a pit of nothingness
Harnessed by my bed covers
The lights stayed off
And I didn't speak much
Sister said she hadn't seen my face
Mother told me to get out of bed

But once I got up and out
Of that strange state
I cleaned the mess in my room
And danced around to a beat
Trying to re-unify reality and me

Once I finally reached some sort of happy
You guys broke down, shook the ground
Pulled this house right from under my feet

You're both faulty
Both turn to me
Only for support and to agree
But you're both wrong
And there's nothing in me
That could smooth over the cracks
In this glass house
It's pretty
But fragile
And cracks have formed
Not from sledgehammers or saw blades
But from tapping and chatter
Silly arguments that don't matter
All rooted in an untimely cause
One of them remembers too well
But she won't let go or move on
The other can't find more words to say 'I'm sorry'
But it doesn't seem to matter how many times they
talk about it
It forever lingers
Pulling all the wrong triggers
Making all my fingers
Contort to make them stay
Pushing and pulling and pinching and curling
One is more flexible than the other
But still has a bigger mouth than her mother
Fingers bent and tongue scalded

I am left with being scolded
Their relationship constantly being unfolded
Torn up
Patched by flimsy cloth
Needle and thread were never enough
Thrown in a fire
Drenched in their blood
Unspoken words and ones spoken too much
Two separate worlds
Two minds disconnected
Two voices that can't seem to find
A certain harmony
I just wish they'd be kind

9.35 p.m.
April 1st, 2019.

Tangled In Blankets

I want to grind
On his lap
Push him down
Kiss his neck
Make my way down his chest
Until I reach his belt
Show him what my mouth can do

Want him to flip me over
Pin my hands down
His hips between mine

Whine beneath him
Scratch at his back

You've Become a Symbol of

You're in my fantasies
I want to use you like a toy
Happy endings
Sit on your lap and not for an innocent cause
Drag your hips across
And breathe kisses into your neck

Desire Tampers

If we fucked would it be too much
And if we don't, will this be enough?
Surely I'll break
The confines
of these friendly times
The line may become a dot to me
If sense doesn't take hold of me
I'll lose my sense of responsibility
I'll show a side that's a little less friendly
And a little more vile
A side of me that makes me worth men's while
A little less smile
And a little more dirty
A part of me that used to control me
Say something I shouldn't
Blurt words that mustn't be uttered
The kind that would open the gates
Let the dam flood
And damn us both.

Guilty Says Me

If I were to die today
Or tomorrow
Or next year
My last words would be
I'm sorry
I'm sorry
I'm so sorry
I'm sorry

Hush Hush

You don't see me as a woman
That's what's going on
What do I have to do
To make you see you're wrong
Should I wear a thong
And see if you'll play along

I want you to show interest
In me
More
I want to make you
Want
More

      -   why is it always older men

Because i'm not sure

Tears in my eyes.
Don't ask me why

bedtime

i want to
dance
on your lap

Anxiety Come Knocking

My heartbeat is pounding in my ears
Thudding in its cage.
And no, it's not for any good reason
It's my anxiety creeping

Over Rated

Alcohol is just a buzz
Adrenaline is just a rush
I would rather take
Two hugs
Or sip on double the tea
In mugs

Vodka is the name of a dog
But it also comes in a shot
Whiskey paired with coke
Its putrid smell could make you choke
Wine comes in red and it comes in white
Peach and cherry flavor rum
Red wine makes cashews taste like dirt
All those together make the floor tremble under
your foot

I'd rather not.
It doesn't make me feel good.

But I still drink. Socially.
And collapse in bed.
I'm left with a headache
And a pained neck.

Under My Skin, On My Nerves –
you're everywhere it hurts

I don't want you
On my mind
I don't want you
In my dreams
I don't want you
Generally

I can only have you so
out of reach
So I'd rather not reach at all

"Maybe you're not on my mind as much as I'm on
yours
Did you think of that maybe?"

Yes I did
All the time
It's what keeps me grounded
Sometimes that means that
my heart gets stepped on
But it's a reminder
That this is all I'll get

I'm looking you in the eyes but you're looking
down to me

You're an incline
I'm just a catastrophe
Don't get me wrong
I don't want you
I don't love
I'm not in love
There is no love here
There is only lust
With a sprinkle of
Vulnerability
Discomfort
Nervousness
Anxiety
Insecurity
Fantasy
Disappointment
Urges
And resentment

I resent you for the way that you make me feel
And that way that you don't make me feel
And for listening but not talking
For pressing buttons I didn't know I had
For-
Oh, and just so you know
If I'm saying nice things

I'm trying to say good bye
If I avoid your question
I want you to ask it again but better
If I jokingly call you names
You got on my nerves
And if I let you into my mind
You'd better fucking be nice

11:15
April 22nd, 2019.

I Have to Loosen My Grip on You

Oh, Gosh
It feels so good
To keep in touch but not talk to you
To feel less and less
Think about you less as time goes by
Be a little less of a mess
Than when we spoke last

Conversation with you now seems impossible
You find new buttons to push and new levers to
pull
A joke becomes a jab
A smile becomes a frown
A stability becomes vulnerability
That leads to my stupidity and ultimately my
uncomfortability
So I push you away
Which is easy because you never tried coming
towards me
Letting go of you is easy because I never had ahold
of you
Let's not forget
You were on my mind
I'm not on yours
You're worth my time
I'm not worth yours
You're a man
And I'm only a girl
You're my so-called friend

I'm just a specimen
And you can't be in a friendship all alone
At least that's not how it's meant to be
But one thing I'm certain of
I need to let go of you
I've got to give up
On this thing I made up
You don't put in the effort
So why should I
Why should I
Because I can't help it
But I have to start
Start stopping
I've got to learn to stop
Stop waiting and trying
And trying to wait
Then failing and planting
Another failed bait
Can't make you start caring
Can't change my fate
All this frustration I'm bearing
Anxiety I'm taming
It's too much and I can't take
it lightly
or slowly
or in small doses to throw me
off the path to panic attacks
to another road with plenty of grass

I don't know what it is anymore
That sends me back to you

When I met you I had no one
Now I have plenty more than you
Yet you're the one I choose
I don't know
I'm so unsure

April 23rd, 2019.

Unsolicited Dreams

Last night I dreamt of you
For the first time in years

–   It's just the idea of being loved that...

writhing

I feel all tingly and that makes me feel lonely don't have anyone to hold me or stroke me or push themselves toward me

April 30th, 2019.

Wishful Thinking

I wonder if anyone ever
Looks for me in the crowd
Thinks about me without my knowledge
Goes back to old texts
Has a glance too many at my old photos
I wonder if
That's possible
If it happens
Or if I'm the only one

I don't want to do anything anymore

Impressive school
Teachers come from places like Liverpool
Parents pay it money out the wazoo
It has a promising exterior
Makes other schools seem inferior
But it robs you of your time
Takes the passion out of your practices

- don't tell me how to do art

May 5th, 2019.

Whose Emotions Am I Feeling?

Whose emotions am I feeling?
It's 3 a.m. the room is dark I should be sleeping
Instead I'm heaving
Whose emotions am I feeling?

All the sudden I'm devastated
Mouth tears open
Cries are whaling out of me. Silently.
My eyes water in a millisecond
Eyebrows furrow as if that's how they're made to
be
Whose emotions am I feeling?

I want to sleep
Not just to shut out the world
But to shut myself out
I have the urge
To do great things
But then on sleep I purge
Whose emotions am I feeling?

Sleep--when life meshes into itself
Folds over itself again and again
Layers and layers until the first one is buried
Like water colors. Translucent I am. I absorb all of
you.

I don't know whose emotions these are anymore.

18

Once I turn 18
I can want who I want
Without the guilt in between
Once I turn 18
I can feel how I feel
I can let myself be
Cut the restraints of being underage me
This number will no longer be a cage

Once I turn 18
I will no longer be prisoner
Once I'm 18

Keep the Bad Dreams Away

When I feel scared and sad
Unstable and down
I listen to people's voices to calm me
Before I sleep
And sometimes during the day, if it's really bad

Strangers
I don't know them in person
They don't know me
I listen to their voices
They have kind faces and speak gently
Sometimes in whispers
It doesn't give me tingles
It just makes me feel more okay
It makes me calmer
At least enough so that I can sleep

Faltering

I thought that I was fixing myself up
Never to be this broken again
But I was just plastering on a strength
That I'd never really obtained
And it falters
Falters
It takes me down with it
Who am I to think
That I can truly be okay

Departure

Don't leave me

If you're not going to stay, don't come near me
If I'm in the way, just tell me.
No body can promise me eternity
Yet I insist on nothing less
Don't make promises you can't keep
Give me an infinity

Don't leave me.

Get out
Come closer
Whisper to me
Hold me
Stop it
You're lying
Your touch isn't everlasting
I'm in an hourglass
Drowning
In every minute passing
You'll fade like the rest of them
You'll leave me they all will
Don't touch me
Come near me
Don't whisper that you'll be here. Always. That's
what you'll say. How can you lie, straight to my
face.

Don't leave me
Or don't leave a trace
Make me forget that you
Ever came my way

Don't leave me
Like they all do
I'm just waiting
To see who's left
I'll be wailing
In my broken bird-nest
Waiting for someone to return
I'll be skeletal before they do
I'll end up leaving someone else too

Look, God, look what you make of us.

> – *whoever is stupid enough to love me*

A Single Thought is Enough to

Saturday.
May 2019.
I had a good day.
I listened to music on my way home.
A lyric triggered a thought.
My stomach tied in a knot.
I got home.
I took off my clothes
I washed my hands
Then a thought popped in my head
I put my hair back in a headband
Two strands of hair I'd left out on purpose
The emotions that escaped
My suppression
Keep pushing them back along with the thoughts
that undress them
They are the depression
Keep pushing forward through the mess that they
made
I keep thinking I got rid of the pain but it was only
delayed
Those two thoughts fell out of my floodgates and I
fell with them
I reached for the soap and my legs caved
Hands clutch the sink knees bent I'm almost on
the floor
I keep thinking why and that I've already done this
before
I thought I fixed it but I don't anymore

Red-faced veins in my eyes glazed you'd be
amazed how quick my facial expression changed
It only took a thought
For me to tie up in knots
And it only took two
To render me hopeless messed up and reckless
Tears they're fucking demons taking all the joy out
of me
Fears that's what they're using to take the life right
out of me
Strength.!
Where's the fucking strength that I'm supposed to
be?.!
Why do I walk with a shake
Why do I enclose a hurricane
Where is the sugarcane when I'm in pain what do I
gain from living it why am I here if not to feel
something fucking great
Why do I make the same mistakes
I'm tired of my sorry ways
I just want to be okay
For real
Not fake
Not in decay
I don't want my pain to be suppressed
I want to put my body and mind to rest
Can't be depressed
I want a break
My heart and soul
Emotions and more
They're no one else's to take

But I don't control them
They control me
And I don't call it guidance It's called fucking
violence Where is all the kindness
I should have for me

I want everybody
To be with me
To be happy
To never leave
To never be ill
To stay with me
To stay
To be here
To stay
Stay.
Don't leave me.!

Then I lathered my hands
To wash my face
Then my hands
Then my feet
Then my hands
Then my flip-flops
Then my hands

And then I laid down again
Tears.
One word that can be read two ways.

With both applied I say tonight I have tears in my
eyes and tears of my heart these tears that I cry are
tearing me apart
Mother and Sister

If one of you ever dies I will follow suit
I'm afraid of death but I'm more afraid of losing
you
There's nothing else to live for

May 23rd, 2019.

Searching

Whenever I open up to someone
They make me want to install thicker bars
Round my mind and my heart
They don't understand or
They don't appreciate
Either way they never hesitate
To make me regret it
Faster than I said it
They don't deserve to hear it or see it
They always crush my fragile spirit

When I try to get close to someone
They make me want to step back a hundred yards
People are ignorant
I feel like I'm from Mars
The only one
The outsider
The disaster without cause
Yes I'm a fucking natural disaster
So watch out
I'm armed

This.

What keeps me afloat?
What keeps me sane?
If I am a boat,
Then the world is my rain.

June 5th, 2019.

Fuck you you're not here.

I know that you don't notice
And I know that you don't care
But just in case you wondered
You're still in my mind
So you're still everywhere

You'll find yourself here
Between lines
Exploding mines
Under my feet

I am absolutely
Undeniably
Ever so tragically
Delusional.

    -   i guess this is sixteen

Bared

This is me
Unapologetically.
And ironically
It's full of "sorry"

Love Like Them

How many fucking people do I have to
Love from afar?
Father was enough
Father was enough, trust me

Don't give me any more
Or rather
Don't take any more from me
How many times
Will this happen with me
I want to love
Unapologetically
Is that too much of me?

It's Only Lust

If you *were* mine
I would be terrified
And in time
I'd leave.

Glass Eyes

At this point I'm just living it up in my imagination
It takes me places I can't ever go
It makes me feel things I'll never know

I'm Trying

Spit that taste of yesterday out my mouth
And try to season today a little better

Not like other little girls

I tried.
I tried to act my own age before when I was little
I couldn't stand the others they were kids to me.
So then I started growing up older than I was
supposed to be
I learned quick things I shouldn't and made
mistakes
Made memories I will never forget. No matter how
hard I try.
I aged strange my face changed body changed but
what stayed the same was people's view of me
I was still a child no matter how I wanted
perceived
They would never treat me equally. Age is just a
number well tell that to my shunner I got no clue
what I'm supposed to do
I tried to be myself and my heart got broken,
I tried to act my age and my peers keep walking or
they're only ever talking
About themselves and their troubles
All their invisible bricks weighing harder on their
shoulders they can't spare you a moment to see the
load that you're holding
I'm tired of losing my sense of self to uphold an
image that I never felt
Soon you can call me dysmorphic, always
changing to appear as who they want be to be...
That person's ideal and what that person approves
of

Always trying to appeal to them
I'm tired of believing them
When they say I should behave this way or that
Maybe they should just treat me with my due
respect
It was not by choice or treason to your society's
norms and expectations that I am the way that I
am
I am more ages than one and I do not wish to be a
nun so do not treat me like one. Or you'll see how
tired I've become.

It's not about you

You text slightly as if not too strong or faded to
lose me but you don't realize that you emotionally
bruise me
But it's me.
I'll take it from you. If that's all you'll give I'll kiss
your hand too.
Because it's me.
The longer I know you, the more unapproachable
you get. I feel it less and less. The comfort and
ease.
It could very well be lots of other things.
That we remain a string of letters to each other
now. That the line has become thinner and thinner
without seeing you in the flesh.
That I'm actually becoming uncomfortable with
myself rather than you.
Because I've been opening up too much to a nut I
can't crack open.
I want this nut to see me and think... Of me.
But it won't.
It cannot be, and it never will.
I keep trying to crack this nut open. Trying to
impress it. For what?
I always say it's because you're my closest friend.
But we both know that's not true.
So, again. For what?
I have to keep going at it. Anything to make you
say *something* that gives me that feeling again.
I want to feel that you're interested in me.

That you admire me. I'm equal. I'm worthy.
I'm funny. I'm sexy. I'm intelligent.
I have yet to feel most of those, but I try... And I
wait.
Sometimes I catch a fish. A small, pitiful fish that I
have to throw back in the water like I
never caught it.
And for one split second. A moment. I feel it. I
don't know what it is... But I feel it. And I'm
addicted to it.
And then the next second, I've disappeared. I do
not exist to you anymore.
I want you to look at me by choice. To ask me
because you feel like it and to answer because you
want to.
I just spoke to you yesterday. I miss you. I missed
you as I was reading what you said, and I missed
you as I replied.
I miss you. You walk on by.

ginger h. goodall

*You're not there for me but at least you make me
tea*

They ask me questions
With no intent to hear the answer
I'm only there
For their own pleasure
Does that sound
Like a friend to you?

      –   *I don't think you know how to*

It runs in the family

Daddy is a poet too!
He wants to make it!
Just like you

I'm sorry darling
I can't give it to him
Just out of the blue
He has to earn it.
Just like you.

Time Is Slipping

I'm getting older

Gray Matter

I am not black
Or white
I am not yellow
Or pink
I am not from Here
Or There
I am not This
Or That

My parents are not divorced
Nor are they Mrs. & Mr.

I do not feel anything
Nor do I feel nothing
I am not calm
Nor am I crying

I am not alive
Nor am I dead
I am all the million things
Inside my head

July 10th, *2019.*

ginger h. goodall

Layers of Humanity

the burdens we bear
we see everywhere
but this is how we escape
and this is how it tastes
black coffee's bitterness
some sugar and milk
sweetness in a glass you'll drink
this is how we cope
and sometimes it leaves us broke
this is the bitterness
the sweetness
the in-between
the struggles and the ease
turn the page please
i call this unity
i call this individuality

this is humanity
this is how we think
and how we feel
can you feel the heartbeats
beating off the page
our hearts are racing beyond its cage
oh our ribs were just made
to block out the pain
but things seem to slither in
fine this way

our hearts are going to cave

bones make up our knuckles
our face and all our troubles
because soon they turn to dust
they wear away at us

but forget all the tragedies
the loose change we can't find
the loose screws in our mind
we won't lose this time
at the end of the day
you can sit at a tray
and drink away
not the wine or champagne
nothing that could numb the pain
no need for intoxication
all we need is the confrontation
of our problems
of our pain
we just need to tell it
not today

so sip gently at your tea, your milk
or your coffee
soft hues of herbs and coffee beans
don't forget the soft creams
all these colors make us
they infiltrate us
we are the warm comfort that slides down our
throat
we are brews and roasts
we are everything that brings us serenity

and everything that don't
we are our successes and the time that we choked
so when you look down at your drink
in your hand in your grip
that's you and your life
you're the one holding it
and you can decide if it burns or it sits
perfectly in your stomach like
you wanted it

and don't you worry
if your face is getting blurry
people decide for you
what defines you
your skin tone
the way words roll off your tongue
or clothes hang off your body
if they try that again
then tell them this without a sorry
if we strip down
all the clothes
all the skin tones
all the things that they say
what is left of us
but bones
that all look the same

people often relate
skeletons
with tons of pain
death, tragedy

but i'm here to say
our skeletons are just one way
that make you and me
one and the same
at the end of the day
at the end of a lifetime
this is how you and me.
we unify

sometime in 2019.

You Are Charming Despite the Ego

I want your company
Without having to ask for it.
I want to be in your presence
And I don't want to talk
I just want to be near you
Until it's much later o'clock

Back to Basics

It's easier
And just makes so much sense
For me to be depressed

I think I'm realizing

It was as I drank a glass of tea
Made by someone else, that had two spoons of
sugar
Which was my usual
And thought it was too sweet
That I realized
I am becoming more
Like my father
With each sip
Slowly but surely
Craving the same constant
Bitterness

And isn't that what
Everyone in this family is
Afraid of?

July 25th, 2019.

Nothing, Nothing...

Oh, I'm wasting away
I'm wasting away
I'm so so so
Sorry
Again today.

ginger h. goodall

to be continued

About the poet

Ginger Goodall has been writing poetry
since childhood, journaling her
personal experiences
to cope with all the big feelings
that she didn't know where else to put.
After finding home
in small town Indiana, USA,
Ginger finally began publishing
her life-long works in hopes that
someone out there
who struggles as she did
picks up this book and
delights in knowing
that they are not alone.